Christmas At Our House

FAMILY HOLIDAY TRADITIONS

Written and Illustrated by
DONNA GREEN

VERMILION

This edition of *Christmas at our House* published in 1998 by
Vermilion, Inc., P.O. Box 176, Cohasset, MA 02025; USA.

If you would like to own a limited-edition, signed & numbered,
reproduction of a painting by artist Donna Green write to
Donna Green, c/o Vermilion, Inc., P.O. Box 176,Cohasset, Ma 02025.

A Rob Fremont Book

Design by Berge Zerdelian
Senior Editor: Susan Watson Moline
Culinary Consultants: Roland Parent, John Parent
Managing Editor: Pati Cockram
Assistant Editors: Oliver Fremont,
Michael Leyden, Sebnem Tokcan
Composition: Garbo Typesetting

ISBN: 1-883746-13-2

Printed and bound in Singapore by Imago Publishing Ltd.

10 9 8 7 6 5 4 3 2 1

For my dad,
who always knows where
to find the best red berries!

Contents

CHRISTMAS IS HERE

LET THE FEAST BEGIN

*H*eap the holly! Wreath the pine!
Train the dainty Christmas vine —
Let the breath of fir and bay
Mingle on this festal day —
Let the cedar fill the air
With its spicy sweetness rare.
Wake the carol — sound the chime —
Welcome! Merry Christmas time!

— HELEN CHASE

Christmas At Our House

*W*hat is it about Christmas that brings such joy? Ribbons and reindeer, cinnamon and secrets? For me, it is the giving. This book is about traditions, perhaps the most enduring of all gifts to our children. Created in your own way, they can be as simple as who gets to lick the spoon. They are the little things we do year after year that knit us together as families and bind us across generations. Especially at Christmas, traditions say, "I love you."

Happy, happy Christmas, that can win us back to the delusions of our childhood days, recall to the old man the pleasures of his youth, and transport the traveler back to his own fireside and quiet home!

– CHARLES DICKENS

The Days
Before Christmas

*F*or children, these days go on forever. For us grown-ups, they fly by with never enough time to accomplish everything. At our house, we try to slow down and savor the anticipation each new day brings. Sledding, skating, and caroling with our children are exhilarating, given enough dry mittens and a steady supply of hot chocolate. Even the busyness of baking, wrapping, and decorating becomes fun when we do it as a family. Only six more days!

*A*mong the cedars, spruces, and hemlocks all was peaceful and quiet.
It was as if they entered a world where strife and man-made problems
were unknown. There was a gentle murmuring among the branches
overhead. The air was filled with the tangy, invigorating fragrance of
the evergreens.
—HAYDN S. PEARSON

O Christmas Tree

One of the best parts of the season is our family outing to Tree Berry Farm to choose our tree. Usually the Sunday before Christmas, my husband Bob and I bundle the children up and we're off! We make a summer outing there too, to pick the blueberries we freeze for Christmas morning breakfast. Now amid snowballs and "Jingle Bells" are evergreens destined for equal greatness. We run from one tree to another, determined to find the most perfect one of all. Seven-year old Monique dislikes the Scotch Pines — they bite, she says. Instead, she wants to take home the saddest-looking tree because nobody else will buy it. Ten-year old Adam likes the Douglas Firs. Me? I like the Balsams because their fragrance lasts. Long ago, I began saving needles from our Christmas trees as keepsakes of special years. The deep woodsy smell of Balsam still lingers in a little round box with a note inside that says, "Adam's First Christmas."

Our family's favorite kind of Christmas tree

_____

_____

A favorite Christmas tree story

_____

_____

_____

_____

_____

A Bird's Christmas Tree

Children enjoy making a Christmas treat for backyard birds. Use cookie cutters to make shapes from bread. Dry the bread shapes in a warm oven for ten minutes, then spread with peanut butter and sprinkle with birdseed, adding cranberry halves for edible color. Hang these treats on evergreen branches for your backyard neighbors.

What an enormous magnifier is tradition! How a thing grows in the human memory and in the human imagination, when love, worship, and all that lies in the human heart, is there to encourage it.

—THOMAS CARLYLE

Hidden Treasures

$\mathcal{A}$ few years ago, I worked at "The Quarterdeck," an antique shop that has been in my friend Joan Noble's family for generations. Originally a lobster pound, it still sits high on wood pilings overlooking the proud fishing fleet of Scituate Harbor. One day, while rummaging through a box of hidden treasures, I discovered a tiny tin mold in the shape of a lobster. I was enchanted and asked Joan, an expert on such things, how it might have been used. "Why, that's for barley pops, of course!" she said. I'd never heard of them, so Joan explained this New England tradition and gave me her own family recipe. Thus began my passion for collecting candy molds, one that Adam and Monique already share!

A favorite recipe or gift to make at Christmas time

_____

_____

_____

_____

BARLEY POPS

2 cups sugar
⅔ cup light corn syrup
¾ cup water

Oil flavors (optional)*
Food coloring (optional)

Blend the sugar, corn syrup, and water in a saucepan and slowly bring the mixture to a boil. When it reaches the hard crack stage or 290°F on the candy thermometer, remove the pan from the heat and stir in a dash of flavoring and color as desired. A few drops of blue or teal coloring will make the finished candy resemble old glass. Pour the hot mixture into glass, ceramic or tin molds, quickly placing the ends of a loop of gold cord or thin ribbon inside the top of the mold before the sugar can harden. When they are filled, carefully move the molds to a cool place for the candy to set. When it finally hardens, a little tug on the cord or ribbon will quickly release the crystalline beauty from the mold. We hang these sparkling light catchers in the kitchen windows, but they also make magical tree ornaments and gifts. And best of all, they fill the house with an incredible aroma.

*If you cannot find oil flavors, you may use vanilla, almond or other various flavors sold in markets.

Deck The Hall

*E*ach year, we unwrap blown glass and antique ornaments as gingerly as we did the very first time. But it's the decorations we gather and make ourselves that I consider our real heirlooms. These arrive all year long — from the garden, the sewing box, and the top of the wood stove. In the summer, Adam grows statice and silver dollars in his garden. He dries them, along with hydrangea, then places them in clusters on the Christmas tree just so. In the fall, Monique and I string cranberries with odd beads and bright trinkets we've collected at yard sales. Come December, the children persuade me to cook up a batch of "barley pops" in their favorite shapes of angels, snowmen, and nutcrackers. Glistening on the tree and in our windows, these hard candy ornaments reflect our joy in just being together.

Our favorite ornaments

_____

_____

_____

How they make me feel

_____

_____

_____

Memories they bring back

_____

_____

_____

How we decorate our tree

_____

_____

_____

Home Sweet Home

*N*estled in the mountains of Vermont sits my cousin Judy's house. It's as welcoming as her hug, as busy as Santa's workshop. Something's always cooking atop the old wood stove, which stands stoutly in the center of her kitchen — usually goodies being put up from her garden. Judy's shelves are laden with homecooked preserves and her beds are piled high with quilts lovingly handcrafted over the long cold winters in Hartland Four-Corners. The delicious aroma of bubbling maple syrup often wafts through the house, enveloping all in its warmth and comfort. After the rich brown liquid is sufficiently cooked down, she will pour it over fresh fallen snow as a special treat for the children. Judy has always known how to make something special out of nothing and takes pride in doing things well. Her home reminds me of a gingerbread house!

Friends we love to visit during the holidays

_____

_____

What I cherish about the way they celebrate Christmas

_____

_____

A favorite recipe from a friend

_____

_____

_____

_____

_____

GINGERBREAD HOUSE

Makes: 1 house and several trees and critters*

5½ cups sifted all purpose flour
1 teaspoon baking soda
1 teaspoon salt
3½ teaspoons ground cinnamon
2½ teaspoons ground ginger
2 teaspoons ground cloves

1 teaspoon ground nutmeg
1 cup vegetable shortening
1 cup sugar
1 cup molasses
1 egg

Preheat oven to 300°F.

Sift all dry ingredients into a large bowl. In a separate bowl beat the shortening and sugar until fluffy. To the sugar mixture add molasses and egg, then combine with the dry ingredients to make a stiff dough. Chill for several hours. Roll dough on a lightly floured surface to ⅛ inch thickness. Cut out house shapes with cookie cutters or a sharp knife. Bake on an ungreased cookie sheet ½ inch apart for 20 minutes or until firm to the touch. Cool on a rack for 5 minutes. Glue house together with icing.

*Cutters for these may be found in most cake decorating stores.

ROYAL ICING

3 egg whites, at room temperature
4 cups confectioners' sugar
½ teaspoon cream of tartar

Beat all ingredients at high speed for up to 10 minutes. Use immediately. Rebeating will not restore texture. Yield: 2½ cups. Make sure you use a grease-free bowl for mixing and cover with a damp cloth to keep the icing from crusting over.

GINGERBREAD MEN

MAKES 12-24

½ cup shortening
½ cup brown sugar
½ cup dark molasses
¼ cup water
2½ cups all-purpose flour
½ teaspoon baking soda

¾ teaspoon grated crystallized ginger
¼ teaspoon allspice
¼ teaspoon nutmeg
½ teaspoon salt
Raisins
Decorator's icing

Preheat oven to 375°F.

Combine shortening, brown sugar, molasses, and water in a large bowl. In another bowl, mix flour, salt, baking soda and spices, and add to the sugar mixture. Blend thoroughly and let chill in the refrigerator for several hours. On a well-floured surface, roll dough to ⅛ inch thickness, or a bit thicker if you like your gingerbread men more rounded and soft. Cut with gingerbread cutters. Use raisins to make eyes and buttons. Place ½ inch apart on an ungreased cookie sheet and bake for 10 to 12 minutes or until firm to the touch. Let cool before your helpers add crooked smiles with icing.

Baking gingerbread perfumes a house like nothing else. It is good eaten warm or cool, iced or plain. And it improves with age, should you be lucky enough or restrained enough to keep it around for any length of time.

—LAURIE COLWIN

Don't Forget The Marshmallows

*M*onique and Adam lumber through the back door, snowsuits bulging with extra layers. Monique, in mittened hands, clutches my old tasseled stocking cap, now balled with snow. Adam pulls off leggings creased with white and heads for the warmth of the kitchen fire. "Mommy, my cheeks sting," announces Monique. "Let me rub them," I say. "When I was little, I always loved that tingly feeling." She looks at me a little doubtfully. The two of them have been sledding down Ash Street all afternoon, just as I used to do. "Hot chocolate will be ready in a minute," I promise. The thought warms my soul. "Don't forget the marshmallows," calls Adam, as if I ever would. I want a frothy white mustache too.

Recipe for our family's favorite wintertime drink

_____

_____

_____

_____

_____

 SPICED PINEAPPLE PUNCH

MAKES ABOUT 8 SERVINGS

3 cups unsweetened pineapple juice
2 cups unsweetened white grape juice
1 cup water
½ of a can (6 ounce) frozen lemonade concentrate,
 thawed (⅓ cup)
¼ cup brown sugar, lightly packed

3 sticks cinnamon, broken
1 teaspoon whole cloves
1 teaspoon whole allspice
Whole cranberries or orange slices
 (optional)

Combine pineapple juice, grape juice, water, lemonade concentrate, and brown sugar in a large saucepan. Make a spice bag by tying cinnamon, cloves, and allspice in a 6-inch square of cotton cheesecloth; add to juice mixture. Bring to boil. Reduce heat, cover, and simmer for 10 minutes. Remove spice bag and discard. Serve in heatproof glasses or punch bowl. Garnish with skewered cranberries or an orange slice, if desired. Sometimes Monique has more garnish than punch.

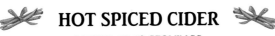

HOT SPICED CIDER

MAKES 10-12 SERVINGS

7 cups apple cider or apple juice
⅓ cup brown sugar, lightly packed
2-3 sticks cinnamon
1 teaspoon whole allspice
1 teaspoon whole cloves

Peel of 1 lemon, cut into strips
1 to 1½ cups rum (optional)
Butter or margarine
Thin apple slices (optional)

Combine apple cider or juice and brown sugar in a large saucepan. Make a spice bag by tying cinnamon, allspice cloves, and lemon peel in a 6-inch square of cotton cheesecloth. Drop spice bag into cider mixture. Bring to boil. Reduce heat, cover, and simmer for 15 minutes. Remove spice bag and discard. Stir in rum. Pour cider mixture into mugs and float a pat of butter or margarine on top. Garnish each serving with one or two thin apple spices, if desired.

 # HOT CRIMSON TODDY

MAKES 10-12 SERVINGS

6 cups cranberry juice cocktail
2 cups water
½ cup sugar
¼ cup lemon juice
Peel of ½ lemon, cut into strips

2 sticks cinnamon
1 teaspoon whole cloves
½ cup bourbon, rum, or orange juice
Lemon peel or orange slices (optional)

Combine cranberry juice cocktail, water, sugar, and lemon juice in a 4-quart saucepan. Make a spice bag by tying cinnamon, lemon peel, and cloves in a 6-inch square of cotton cheesecloth. Drop spice bag into fruit mixture. Bring to boil. Reduce heat, cover, and simmer for 10 minutes. Remove spice bag and discard. Add bourbon, rum, or orange juice. Pour into a heatproof carafe or mugs. Garnish each cup with a strip of lemon peel or an orange slice, if desired.

 # MOCHA EGG NOG

MAKES 6-8 SERVINGS

1 cup milk
1 cup light cream
2 beaten egg yolks
2 tablespoons sugar

Ground nutmeg
2 cups espresso or double-strength coffee
Whipped cream
Brandy or rum (optional)

Combine milk and light cream in a medium heavy saucepan. Combine egg yolks, sugar, and a dash of nutmeg in a bowl, and add to milk. Cook and stir over medium heat till mixture coats a metal spoon. Add coffee to mixture in saucepan, beating with a whisk to combine. Top each serving with whipped cream; you may also add a shot of brandy or rum and sprinkle with ground nutmeg.

The Scent Of Christmas

*F*rom the moment the tree comes inside, it's Christmas. The dense, green fragrance of Balsam — it was my turn to choose this year — permeates the house and once again transports me back to my childhood. As soon as the tree is decorated, I gather Monique up in my lap. "When I was a little girl, my favorite thing to do was lie down under the tree and look up through the branches," I tell her. "Let's do it now, Mommy!" she exclaims. Monique and I lie head-to-head beneath the tree and breathe in the magic of Balsam. Together we gaze up through a Christmas fairyland, imaginations climbing starry boughs to the top of our own little world.

How our home changes on the day the Christmas tree is brought inside

_____

_____

_____

What I did on that day as a child

_____

_____

_____

What I hope my children will treasure and preserve for their own little ones

_____

_____

_____

_____

_____

Sweet Centerpieces

"*A*pples, I said I wanted apples. These are pomegranates." At the very word, Monique began to giggle. "Pome-what?" she asked. "Pomegranates," I answered, a little exasperated. I'd sent both children to the grocery store with Bob for the apples we needed for our tabletree. At Christmas time, our tables are heaped with wrapping and ribbon, special recipes and endless lists of things to do. Somehow a centerpiece brings order to it all. Now what were we going to do without apples? "That's easy," piped up Adam. "Use pomegranates instead." And so we did, along with boxwood and the yarrow we'd collected on the beach that summer. Now every year, we've got the only pomegranate tree in town.

My favorite centerpiece

_____

_____

_____

How we love to decorate our home

_____

_____

_____

Accidental happenings that have become family traditions

_____

_____

_____

_____

_____

Friends Indeed

"Let's have a tree-trimming party at your house!" The suggestion came from my dear pal Judy, who knew that I needed some extra cheer one particular year. Why not, I thought. I would supply the ornaments and everyone else would supply dinner. Judy volunteered to bring her legendary carrot cake, as well as popcorn for stringing. "Leave all the details to me," she insisted. So the next day, up I went to the attic and dragged down every ornament I could find. Sure enough, friends arrived right on schedule, as if the whole thing had been planned for weeks. The dinner was a feast, of course, and the tree exquisite. But best of all were my friends. They knew that what I needed most was Christmas.

The kindest deed anyone ever did for our family

_____

_____

_____

_____

A present I once received that I can say was truly from the heart

_____

_____

_____

_____

What a friend once taught me

_____

_____

_____

_____

*R*ings and jewels are not gifts, but apologies for gifts.
The only gift is a portion of thyself.

— RALPH WALDO EMERSON

A Cookie Swap

Spritz cookies, chocolate shortbread, meringue kisses — I wish I had time to make everyone's favorite. Instead, I invite five or six friends to an old-fashioned "cookie swap." Each person brings two dozen of a favorite holiday cookie and the recipe that goes with it. Then, over an informal cup of tea, we trade cookies, as well as news. Each of us ends up with a variety of homemade specialties fit to display on any Christmas table. And when my Uncle Slim asks how I found the time to do so much baking, I just smile.

My favorite Christmas cookie recipes

Simple Pleasures

"My basket's for Mrs. Tuthill," Monique announces proudly. "See, Mommy? Look what I did." Caramels, fudge, and gingerbread men with silly smiles are stuck in every which way amid packets of homemade granola, bundles of cinnamon sticks, and cutouts from the "keepers" of last year's Christmas cards. "Here's the bow," Adam chimes in, knocking over a blue pottery bowl and sending granola flying. "It's perfect," I tell them. "Monique, do you know why we're doing this for Mrs. Tuthill?" "Because she doesn't feel well, and it's Christmas." She disappears for just a minute and returns with the little potpourri sachet she made yesterday out of scraps of red satin. "Here, Mommy," she says. "Let's put this in too. I want Mrs. Tuthill to find a new treasure every day."

The person with whom my family most enjoys sharing the bounty of Christmas

_____

_____

_____

Some of the simple gifts we enjoy making for special friends

_____

_____

_____

_____

ALMOND CRUNCH GRANOLA
YIELD: 3 CUPS

2 cups oat flakes and wheat flakes mixed
1 cup almonds, coarsely chopped
¼ cup pure maple syrup

⅓ cup light vegetable oil
¼ teaspoon sea salt
½ teaspoon vanilla

Mix all the ingredients together. Spread thinly on a cookie sheet. Bake 20 to 25 minutes at 325° to 350°F, or until lightly browned. Variation: Add other nuts and seeds, such as sesame seeds, chestnuts, cashews, pecans, walnuts. Use honey in place of maple syrup. If you like almonds, you'll love this one.

Sleigh Ride

Come with me,
You're going on a sleigh ride,
At my side
Through the falling snow.

Take my hand,
We're going on a joy ride,
Laughing
Everywhere we go.

Side by side,
We'll soon be gliding through the snow,
Sleigh bells
Caroling along.
Hear them ring —
Someday we'll be remembering
The way they played
Our song.

Hand in hand,
We're going on a sleigh ride.
Be my guide
Through the drifting snow.

Cheek to cheek,
We're going on a sleigh ride.
Winter
Is the warmest time I know.

—R. A. FREMONT

At the break of Christmas Day,
Through the frosty starlight ringing,
Faint and sweet and far away,
Comes the sound of children singing,
Chanting, singing,
"Cease to mourn
For Christ is born
Peace and joy to all men bringing."

—MARGARET DELAND

House To House

"*M*ommy, where do we go first? When does Jenny come to our house? When's the Swap? When do we go to Timmy's house? Can't we go yet?"

The best thing about the House-to-House Dinner is that it enables us each year to sample the holiday treats and decorations of our friends, as they do ours, with minimum fuss. In fact, I've always said that this New England tradition is the most fun and festive of all the holiday parties. We begin at one house for drinks and appetizers, move on to another for the main course, and end at yet another for dessert and coffee.

Friends who make Christmas doubly special

_____

_____

_____

_____

_____

The best Christmas party I ever attended

_____

_____

_____

_____

_____

*N*ow Christmas is come,
Let's beat up the drum,
And call all our neighbors together,
And when they appear,
Let us make them such cheer
As will keep out the wind and the weather.

—WASHINGTON IRVING

Yankee Swap

*T*his year we added an old-time Yankee Swap to our House-to-House Dinner. Every guest brings a wrapped gift to the last house, usually something silly and inexpensive, and places it under the Christmas tree. Then all the guests draw numbers. Guest Number One chooses a gift and opens it. A sprig of mistletoe tied with red satin cording! Guest Number Two chooses another gift from the heap and opens it. A history of the French Foreign Legion. Guest Number Two has no use for that but big plans for mistletoe, so he swaps with Guest Number One. As each gift is opened, it can be swapped for any that have preceded it. When the last guest has swapped, Guest Number One can choose from the entire array. Next year Adam will know to avoid the package with the blinking red nose!

Our family's favorite gift-giving tradition

_____

_____

_____

_____

The best party story in our family's lore

_____

_____

_____

_____

_____

An embarrassing moment

_____

_____

_____

_____

At Christmas play and make good cheer,
For Christmas comes but once a year.

                                  —THOMAS TUSSER

Dark and dull night fly hence away
And give the honor to this day
That sees December turned to May . . .

                             —ROBERT HERRICK

Winter Wonderland

"Dad, my feet will look like tuna fish sandwiches," Monique said, a little exasperated. "Hold still silly;" Bob replied, "if you want to get out on the duck pond to skate we have to get Mom's old skates on nice and snug! The extra socks will make them fit and the bread bags will keep your feet dry and make the skates go on more easily." Monique's attention was now on the Webster twins matching glide for glide. Ashley was still on double runners earnestly pushing a chair to maintain balance. She looked a bit nervous as three junior high boys wove in and around her with their hockey sticks. Adam looked on in envious awe. As his face lit up with new purpose, I knew there would be an addition to his Christmas wish list.

My favorite outdoor activity at Christmas time

_____

_____

_____

_____

The first time I experienced snow

_____

_____

_____

Something I've never tried but would like to (maybe)

_____

_____

_____

Children At Heart

*T*here's something about Christmas that brings out the child in each of us. Perhaps it's the perfect present in the perfect hiding place that puts the twinkle in our eyes, the mischief in our minds. Take Roland, my father-in-law, for example. He believes in what he calls "cheat gifts," the ones he hopes to open before Christmas morning. The fact that we don't have any of those around our house has never discouraged him from making trouble. "It's big," he says. "It's shiny. It jingles. I know right where it is. Come on, don't you want to take a little peek?" Oh, all right. Maybe a little one!

How I felt as a child awaiting Christmas

_____

_____

_____

The lengths I have to go to hide the presents

_____

_____

_____

Christmas Mystery

There's one more thing, I'm sure of it . . .
Can you figure out just where?

Let's see, I think it's up a stair
And in a room that has a bear.

Once on a cold and rainy night,
As I passed by to warm my room,

It gave me such a shocking fright;
Best to put it out of sight.

Love,
Mom

—ANON

Finishing Touches

*L*ast Christmas, my friend and confidant Sally — who, by the way, helps hold my life together by picking up stray socks and bending where my back will no longer let me go, somehow knowing just where to fill in — stopped by for her weekly visit. She was astonished to find my seven-year-old daughter's room in immaculate condition. The bed was made, shoes were lined up against the wall, and all fifty-eight stuffed friends were neatly lined up on the bed looking as though they were about to sing Handel's Messiah. Hallelujah! "Monique, what happened to your room," asked Sally, amazed. "Well, I don't want Santa to think I'm messy!" replied Monique who then ran out of the room. As she reached the bottom of the stairs, Sally heard her add, "Just don't open my closet."

What my children never forget to do just before Christmas

_____

_____

_____

Last minute preparations I especially enjoy

_____

_____

_____

When I think about the days before Christmas I most like to recall

_____

_____

_____

_____

*L*et my dolls be made of rags,
Fireman hats of paper bags.
Just write "love" on the Christmas tags;
That's what I want for Christmas.

—IRVING CAESAR

Christmas Is Here

*A*t last, it's Christmas Eve. Adam and Monique are tucked in bed and, with the exception of the dollhouse Bob is assembling, all of the presents are wrapped. This is the moment I savor each year. With hymns from the Pageant still ringing in my ears, I sit back with a mug of hot cider and contemplate Christmases past. I go over them in my mind, one by one, humbled again by our many blessings.

Christmas Pageant

For as long as I can remember my family has gathered for the Christmas Eve Pageant at church. I recall as a little girl wearing a long white robe, sparkling gold halo, and lopsided wings of tinfoil that refused to stay upright. My brothers and sister were in it too, as a shepherd and children of Bethlehem. A dear neighbor all of us children knew as Auntie Chris directed the Pageant each year, doing everything from bending coathangers into wings to fastening beards on kings. Over the years, her devotion to the church, and especially to us children, brought her into spiritual contact with nearly every family in our congregation.

I was around nine years old when Auntie Chris passed away. She had always been there, like an angel, teaching responsibility and commitment by her every act. The Pageant had been the center of my Christmas, even as a child. Now who would direct it? Years later, a little voice inside me said, "I'll do it!" I was scared, but in the end, I realized that Auntie Chris had not really left us at all. Still in my heart, she had continued to show the way.

Blessings we are thankful for

_____

_____

The ceremony I cherish most

_____

_____

Our hopes for Christmases to come

_____

_____

Christmas Carol

The kings they came from out the south,
All dressed in ermine fine;
They bore Him gold and chrysoprase,
And gifts of precious wine.

The shepherds came from out the north,
Their coats were brown and old;
They brought Him little new-born lambs —
They had not any gold.

The wise men came from out the east,
And they were wrapped in white;
The star that led them all the way
Did glorify the night.

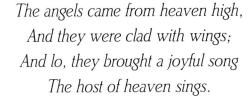

The angels came from heaven high,
And they were clad with wings;
And lo, they brought a joyful song
The host of heaven sings.

The kings they knocked upon the door,
The wise men entered in,
The shepherds followed after them
To hear the song begin.

The angels sang through all the night
Until the rising sun,
But little Jesus fell asleep
Before the song was done.

— SARA TEASDALE

The children were nestled all snug in their beds,
While visions of sugar-plums danced in their heads . . .
— CLEMENT CLARKE MOORE

Christmas Eve

The fire has settled into a soothing crackle, and we snuggle on the sofa. We've walked home from the Pageant, shepherd and angel in the starry night, and have set up my mother's creche once again on the mantle. Our stockings have been hung by the chimney with care, just as Bob read they would be, and there is only one thing left to do. Adam and Monique draw up close, laboring over each word.

Dear Santa, Here are some sugar cookies for you and carrots for your reindeer. How's Rudolph? The biggest carrot is for him. Thank you for everything. By the way, I hope you remember my hockey stick. Your pal, Adam.

Dear Santa, this is Cloud, my stuffed dog. She always sleeps with me, but tonight she wants to see you. Thank you for the presents and have a good trip. Love, Monique. P.S. The biggest carrot is for Dancer.

Christmas Eve at our house

_____

_____

_____

Our tucking-in tradition on Christmas Eve

_____

_____

Letters left for Santa

_____

_____

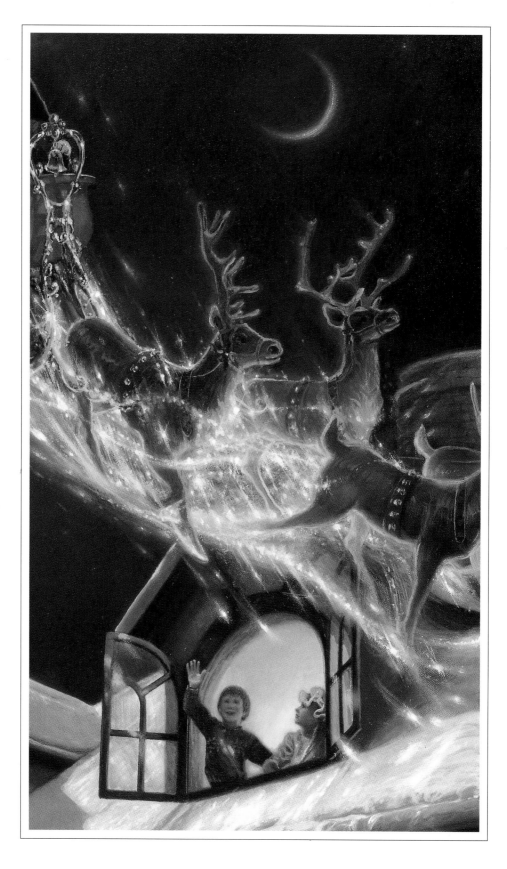

Not believe in Santa Claus! You might as well not believe in fairies!

– FRANCIS P. CHURCH

Sly Santa Claus

All the house was asleep and the fire burning low,
When, from far up the chimney came down a "Ho! ho!"
And a little round man, with a terrible scratching,
Dropped into the room with a wink that was catching.
Yes, down he came, bumping and thumping and jumping,
And picking himself up without sign of a bruise!

"Ho! ho!" he kept on as if bursting with cheer,
"Good children, gay children, glad children, see here!
I have brought you fine dolls, and gay trumpets, and rings,
Noah's arks, and bright skates, and a host of good things!
I have brought a whole sackful, a packful, a hackful!
Come hither, come hither, come hither and choose!"

"Ho! ho! What is this? Why they all are asleep!
But their stockings are up, and my presents will keep!
So, in with the candies, the books and the toys;
All the goodies I have for the good girls and boys.
I'll ram them, and jam them, and slam them, and cram them;
All the stockings will hold while the tired youngsters snooze."

All the while his round shoulders kept ducking and ducking;
And his little fat fingers kept tucking and tucking;
Until every stocking bulged out on the wall,
As if it were bursting, and ready to fall,
And then, all at once, with a whisk and a whistle,
And twisting himself like a tough bit of gristle,
He bounced up again, like the down of a thistle.
And nothing was left but the prints of his shoes.

— Mrs. C.S. Stone

Christmas Morning

*C*hristmas mornings when I was a little girl I used to look out my bedroom window to the Thompsons' for what seemed like hours. Once the Thompsons' lights were on, we could get up. Not until then. One particular year, my brother and I made a plan with Dougie Thompson. He would flick on his bedroom light at four a.m. The ruse worked and we were well into our presents before Mom and Dad realized what time it was!

"Dad, Mom . . . Dad!" Adam snaps me to the present. "You've got to get up! He came! Santa came!" There's no choice but to dash downstairs. Every year, we try to open presents one at a time, but it never lasts more than one round. It's chaos, with waist-high wrapping paper that I try to keep out of the fireplace. My favorite presents are always the ones from the children — our house in clay, a popsicle-stick lady with green hair. Cloud always gets a present too. This year it's a bright red collar with a note from Santa himself.

Who always wakes up first

_____

_____

The best present Santa ever brought

_____

_____

Our best Christmas morning

_____

_____

_____

Christmas morning when I was a child

_____

_____

_____

BLUEBERRY FRENCH TOAST

6 thick slices of white or Challah bread
4 eggs
1 cup milk
1 teaspoon vanilla extract

1 teaspoon salt
2 tablespoons butter, at room temperature
Confectioners' sugar

In a 13″ x 9″ x 2″ baking dish, lay the bread flat in a single layer. Beat the eggs, milk, vanilla and salt together in a bowl, and pour the mixture over the bread. Turn the bread so the mixture covers both sides. Cover dish with plastic wrap and refrigerate overnight to save time in the morning. Next morning preheat oven to 375°F. Grease a baking sheet with butter. Place bread on the baking sheet, transfer to oven, and bake for 10 minutes. Turn bread over and continue baking for another 10 minutes or until golden brown on both sides. Remove bread from the oven and halve it diagonally. Sprinkle with sugar and serve with blueberry sauce.

Blueberry Sauce

1 cup sugar
1 pint blueberries, picked over

Juice of 1 lemon

In a saucepan, combine the sugar and lemon juice and cook over low heat until the sugar begins to turn liquid. Add the blueberries, stir well, and continue cooking over low heat for 10 minutes or until the blueberries soften and form a sauce. Spoon over French toast and serve at once. You may substitute frozen blueberries, especially if you went on a berry-picking outing with your children last summer and announced that you would freeze your harvest for Christmas morning.

EGGS ROLAND

Egg(s)
Bacon
Butter

Salt and pepper
Basil, chives, and chopped parsley

Prehat oven to 325°F.
Grease bottom of muffin pan. Saute or lightly broil strips of bacon. Line the sides of each muffin cup with the bacon. Pour one egg into each cup. Ladle 1 teaspoon melted butter over each egg, sprinkle with salt, pepper, basil, chives and chopped parsley. Bake for about 10 minutes or until eggs are set. Turn them out onto rounds of toast or English muffins. Can be served with Hollandaise Sauce. Who's Roland? Why, my father-in-law of course, as well as chef extraordinaire.

*M*ay you have the gladness of Christmas which is hope; the spirit of
Christmas which is peace; the heart of Christmas which is love.

—ADA V. HENDRICKS

Christmas Past

Over blueberry French toast at breakfast, I tell Adam and Monique the story they never tire of. When I was a little girl, one Christmas was particularly lean. We didn't even have a tree. My sister Sharline wanted only one thing — a Chatty Cathy doll. On Christmas Eve, my mother decided she was going to get that doll no matter what. Pooling our money, we came up with the $14.98 needed and piled into the Pontiac. Hardly anything was open, but my mother had a hunch that the shop at Nantasket Beach might be. It was just closing, but she begged the shopkeeper to let her in just for a minute, just to get the Chatty Cathy for her little girl.

We started home with our purchase, but suddenly my mother pulled off to the side of the road. Ahead of us was a darkened Christmas tree lot, the owner gone home. Barely visible was a sign on the ground, "Trees Reduced-$3." My mother turned to us and said, "Wait here. I'll be right back." She jumped out, ducked under the rope that encircled the lot, and tucked a three-dollar IOU note under the sign. We couldn't believe our eyes! Then she grabbed a tree and threw it in the trunk of the car. "Now he won't have to throw this one away," she exclaimed.

Our family's most amazing Christmas story

_____

_____

_____

_____

_____

I can't help but smile when I remember

_____

_____

_____

_____

This is Christmas Day, the anniversary of the world's greatest event. To one day all the early world looked forward; to the same day, the latter world looks back. That day holds time together.

— ALEXANDER SMITH

Let The Feast Begin

The turkey went in hours ago, its distinctive smell now in every nook and cranny of the house. Children wander in and out of the kitchen, asking if dinner will ever be ready, and we shoo them away. At last, the big moment arrives. We all gather at the table and give thanks for our family love, which grows deeper and richer every year. And now let's eat!

Pass the Gravy

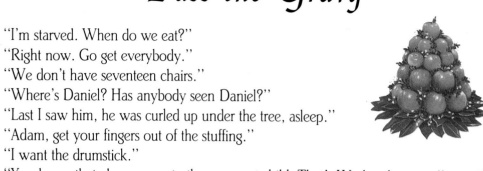

"I'm starved. When do we eat?"

"Right now. Go get everybody."

"We don't have seventeen chairs."

"Where's Daniel? Has anybody seen Daniel?"

"Last I saw him, he was curled up under the tree, asleep."

"Adam, get your fingers out of the stuffing."

"I want the drumstick."

"You know that always goes to the youngest child. That's Wesley this year."

"Don't let my cranberries touch my mashed potatoes. Aw, Dad!"

"Where did Monique go? She hardly ate a thing."

"And Ashley. Where did she go?"

"Don't worry about them. They're up in Monique's room playing with their new dolls."

"I've got dibs on the last piece of Grandma's Heavenly Pie!"

"Wesley, I'll trade you my piece of pie for the drumstick!"

A Christmas menu to remember

_____

_____

_____

_____

_____

_____

_____

_____

_____

Welcome guests

_____

_____

_____

_____

_____

_____

_____

_____

At Christmastime the kitchen becomes the center of our house.

—BARBARA MILO OHRBACH

ZUCCHINI SQUARES
MAKES 48 PIECES

3 cups thinly sliced zucchini
4 eggs, slightly beaten
1 cup Bisquick mix
½ cup finely chopped onion
½ cup vegetable oil
½ cup grated Parmesan cheese

1 clove garlic, finely chopped
2 tablespoons snipped parsley
½ teaspoon oregano
½ teaspoon salt
⅛ teaspoon pepper

Preheat oven to 350°F.
Mix all ingredients well and spread in a 13″ x 9″ x 2″ pan. Bake for 25 to 30 minutes until golden brown. Let cool and cut into 2″ x 1″ pieces. Recipe can easily be doubled, which is important when you see how quickly these gems are gobbled up.

CRAB DIP

1 can (6 ounces) crab meat
1 package (8 ounces) cream cheese
¼ cup sour cream
1 tablespoon milk

1 tablespoon lemon juice
2 tablespoons thinly sliced green onion tops
1 small clove garlic, minced
Salt and pepper

Beat together cream cheese and sour cream. Add other ingredients and mix. Season with salt and pepper. Cover and refrigerate 2 hours. Serve with a platter of raw vegetables or crackers. The vegetables will make everyone think they're being good.

ASPARAGUS, HAM AND CHEESE ROLL-UPS
YIELDS ABOUT 36 PIECES

6 slices boiled ham
1 package (8 ounces) cream cheese

6 cooked asparagus spears
Dijon style mustard

Spread mustard and creamed cheese on sliced ham. Wrap each asparagus spear with ham and cut into ½ inch lengths. Secure with toothpick. Cover and refrigerate for ½ hour.

Recipes At Our House

What makes Christmas dinner so special is the variety of recipes that comprise this sumptuous spread. It isn't just Grandma's Heavenly Pie, it's the fresh sage that Adam grows in his garden for the stuffing, the gingerbread men Monique helps me bake. It's everyone contributing.

Our favorite family feast recipes

_____

_____

_____

_____

_____

_____

_____

_____

_____

Here's my secret recipe

_____

_____

_____

_____

_____

Oh, could we keep the Christmas thrill,
The goad of gladness and good will,
The lift of laughter and the touch
Of kindled hands that utter much . . .
— ANGELA MORGAN

SANTA SOUP
SERVES 12

½ pound ditalini or tubettini or other small macaroni
  products
½ pound shelled uncooked shrimp, chopped medium
8 cups chicken stock
1 can (16 ounces) whole peeled tomatoes, drained,
  chopped coarsely
1 cup dry white wine

2 medium onions, chopped
4 cloves garlic, crushed
5 tablespoons olive oil
6 tablespoons chopped parsley
1½ teaspoon oregano
Salt and pepper to taste
Grated Parmesan cheese

Cook the macaroni in a pan of boiling salted water with a few drops of oil for 10-12 minutes. Drain
well. Heat oil in a deep pan, add onions and saute 2-3 minutes. Add garlic, tomatoes, and half of parsley, cover and steam over low heat for 8-10 minutes. Stir in stock, wine, oregano, salt and pepper and
bring to a boil. Reduce heat, cover and simmer for 20 minutes. Add macaroni and shrimp and simmer
an additional 6-8 minutes. Serve sprinkled with remaining parsley and Parmesan cheese. Adam says
the color of this soup reminds him of Santa.

CHRISTMAS BOUILLON
YIELDS 10 PORTIONS

1½ quart chicken broth
1 quart tomato juice
¾ cup chopped celery
1 small onion, chopped
¾ cups cooked rice

1 teaspoon sugar
1 bay leaf
½ teaspoon salt
1 tablespoon lemon juice

Simmer all ingredients except lemon juice and rice together until vegetables are soft. Strain and add
lemon juice. Add cooked rice. Bring to a boil and keep warm. Monique calls this delicious tomato
broth "Christmas soup."

WALDORF SALAD

SERVES 12

6 medium apples
1 cup diced celery
1 cup raisins
¾ cup mayonnaise
½ teaspoon cinnamon
½ teaspoon ground nutmeg

1 ½ cups pecans
¼ cup maple syrup
2 tablespoons butter
1 can (11 ounces) mandarin
    orange segments (optional)

Preheat oven to 350°F.
Melt butter in saucepan and blend with maple syrup and pecans. Spread on oiled cookie sheet and bake for 15 minutes. While this cools, core and dice unpeeled apples and sprinkle them with lemon juice to prevent darkening. Mix apples, celery, raisins, mayonnaise, cinnamon, and nutmeg. You may also add one 11-ounce can of mandarin orange segments, if desired. Fold nut mixture into fruit just before serving.

A cherished holiday recipe

_____

_____

_____

_____

_____

_____

_____

_____

OYSTER STUFFING

(will fill a 12-pound turkey)

8 cups soft bread cubes (about 12 slices bread)
2 cups (16 ounces) fresh oysters, drained and chopped
or 2 cans (8 ounces) oysters, drained and chopped
2 sticks butter
1½ cups chopped celery (stalks and leaves)
¾ cup finely chopped onion

2 tablespoons finely chopped parsley
1 teaspoon dried thyme leaves
1 teaspoon ground sage
1 teaspoon salt
½ teaspoon pepper

Cook celery and onion in butter in a large skillet, stirring frequently until onion is tender. In a deep bowl place bread cubes, celery, onion and spices; mix thoroughly. Last of all add oysters. Stuff turkey just before roasting. Mmmmmmmmmmm!

ROAST TURKEY

SERVES 12

10 to 12 pound turkey
2 small carrots
2 sticks celery

1 medium onion
½ cup of water

Set out a shallow roasting pan with rack and preheat oven to 325°F.

Rinse turkey and pat dry with absorbent paper. Rub cavity of turkey lightly with salt, if desired. Do not salt cavity if turkey is to be stuffed. Important: stuff turkey just before roasting, not ahead of time. Fill wishbone area with stuffing first. Fasten neck skin to back with skewer. Fold wings across back with tips touching. Fill body cavity lightly; stuffing will expand while cooking. Tuck drumsticks under band of skin at tail or tie together with heavy string, then tie to tail. Place turkey, breast side up, on rack in roasting pan. Brush with melted butter. Add carrots, celery, onion, and ½ cup of water. Roast uncovered for approximate cooking time printed on turkey wrap. When it begins to turn golden, loosely cover turkey with aluminum foil.

Turkey is done when the meat thermometer placed in the thigh muscle registers 180°F. Remove turkey from oven, cover with foil, and allow to stand for at least 30 minutes before serving. Serve stuffing separately. Remove leftover stuffing from turkey. Leftover turkey meat should be removed from bones. Cool stuffing, turkey meat and any gravy promptly. Refrigerate separately.

TURKEY GRAVY
ABOUT 4 CUPS

Remove roasted turkey from pan and place on warm plate, cover with foil, and keep warm. Remove carrots, celery and onion, if used. Leaving brown residue in pan, pour drippings into bowl. Skim off some of fat that rises to surface and discard. The meat juices (drippings) that remain become part of gravy. Measure into roasting pan 2 cups drippings, warm or cool, and 2 cups water. Return pan to heat and cook rapidly, stirring constantly. Scrape bottom and sides of pan to blend in brown residue. Mix 2 tablespoons corn starch with an equal amount of cold water, mix until smooth, and add to hot liquid. Cook until sauce thickens. Serve hot.

ORANGE CRANBERRY SAUCE
MAKES ABOUT 4 CUPS

1 pound (4 cups) fresh cranberries
2 cups sugar

½ cup water
Juice and rind of two large oranges

Pick over the cranberries and remove any that are shriveled or discolored. Use the coarse side of the grater to grate oranges. Take care not to remove too much of the white pith. Cut oranges in half and squeeze them for juice. Combine all ingredients in a saucepan. Cook uncovered for 10 minutes or until cranberry skins pop, stirring once or twice. Remove from heat, cool. Cover and refrigerate.

SNOWFLAKE BISCUITS
YIELD: ABOUT 1 DOZEN BISCUITS

1¾ cups all-purpose flour
2½ teaspoons baking powder
½ teaspoon salt

⅓ cup shortening
¾ cup milk

Preheat oven to 450°F.
Mix flour, baking powder, and salt. Cut shortening into flour mixture with a pastry blender or two knives until mixture resembles fine crumbs. Stir in just enough milk so dough leaves side of bowl and rounds up into a ball. Turn dough onto lightly floured surface. Knead gently 12 times. Roll to ½ inch thickness and cut with 2-inch biscuit cutter. Place on ungreased cookie sheet about 1 inch apart. Bake until golden brown, 10 to 12 minutes. Immediately remove from cookie sheet.

Upstairs At Play

*A*mid the din at the table, I notice Monique sliding down her chair. Actually, it was the rustle in her green taffeta skirt that gave her away. I watch as she tiptoes up behind Ashley, timidly taps her on the shoulder, and whispers something through a cupped hand. Ashley looks at her mother, who nods, and the two little girls go up the stairs hand-in-hand. I know what they're up to, just as Ashley's mother does. The grown-up dinner conversation has turned to a dull buzz and cousins are slipping away, one by one, to play. There's something about new dolls that bridges any gulf between little girls. They escape to their own enchanted world of bonnets and booties, cradles and croons.

How we celebrated Christmas Day when I was young

_____

_____

_____

My happiest ever Christmas Day celebration

_____

_____

_____

My warmest recollection of my family on Christmas Day

_____

_____

_____

_____

_____

There is no Christmas like a home Christmas with your dad and mother, sis and brother there. With their hearts humming at your home-coming, and that merry Yuletide spirit in the air.

— CARL SIGMAN

CANDIED ORANGE CARROTS
8 SERVINGS

½ stick of butter
24 small sliced carrots (about 3 pounds)
1 cup brown sugar, firmly packed

½ cup orange juice
2 tablespoons honey

Preheat oven to 350°F.
Butter a shallow baking dish.
Wash and pare or scrape carrots. Slice and cook in shallow water over medium heat 12 to 15 minutes, or until just tender (do not overcook). Drain and keep warm. Heat butter in a skillet over low heat. Blend in brown sugar, orange juice, and honey. Cook over medium heat, stirring constantly, until sugar is dissolved and mixture bubbles. Drain carrots and place in the baking dish. Pour sugar mixture over carrots and bake about 10 minutes or until carrots are completely glazed. Baste occasionally. Can be frozen and re-heated. There is probably no more popular vegetable with children.

CREAMED ONIONS WITH WALNUTS
SERVES 6-8

2 medium red onions, peeled and thickly sliced
2 medium yellow onions, peeled and sliced as above
1 cup milk
2 tablespoons cornstarch
3 tablespoons butter

⅛ teaspoon grated nutmeg
⅛ teaspoon ground cinnamon
3 tablespoons grated Parmesan cheese
2 tablespoons fine bread crumbs
¼ cup chopped walnuts

Preheat oven to 400°F.
In a saucepan, just submerge onions in cold water, cover and boil for 2-3 minutes. Drain off the water. Return onions to the pan, add milk and 4 tablespoons water. Cover and simmer 10-15 minutes or until onions are tender. Mix cornstarch to a smooth paste with a little extra milk. Add paste to onions and stir over medium heat until boiling. Add 2 tablespoons butter, salt and pepper, nutmeg, and cinnamon. Pour onion mixture into a 2-quart baking dish. Sprinkle cheese and bread crumbs over dish. Sprinkle chopped walnuts over bread crumbs and cheese. Melt the remaining tablespoon of butter and dribble over the top. Bake 25 minutes or until golden brown.

REAL MASHED POTATOES
8 SERVINGS

8 medium potatoes
Boiling salted water
¼ pound (1 stick) melted butter

1 cup hot light cream
Salt and pepper to taste

Peel potatoes and cut into pieces. Cover with boiling salted water and cook covered until they are tender but not mushy. Drain thoroughly. Return the potatoes to the pan and shake over low heat to dry. Mash the potatoes using a potato ricer, potato masher, food mill, or electric mixer. Return to the pan and place over low heat. Beat in the butter and add light cream little by little, beating constantly with a wooden spoon or an electric beater. Season with salt and pepper. Pass the gravy, please.

BUTTERNUT SQUASH
12 SERVINGS

6 pounds butternut squash
1 stick butter (¼ pound), melted
4 teaspoons brown sugar
Dash cinnamon & nutmeg

½ teaspoon salt
¼ teaspoon pepper
Milk

Peel the squash, split in half lengthwise, and remove seeds. Cut into large cubes (about 2″ square). Place in a saucepan with boiling salted water, cover, return to a boil and cook over medium heat about 25 minutes until you can just pierce squash with a fork. Drain, remove the cover, and cook a few minutes to evaporate any excess water. Mash squash, add butter, sugar, salt and pepper, and warm milk, if needed. Its buttery, smooth consistency makes this dish an excellent ''comfort food,'' perfect for a holiday feast.

BRUSSELS SPROUTS WITH CHIVES
6 SERVINGS

1 pound Brussels sprouts, trimmed
¼ cup (½ stick) butter
2 tablespoons chopped chives
3 teaspoons lemon zest

2 teaspoons fresh (or ½ teaspoon dried) dill weed
½ teaspoon salt
¼ teaspoon pepper

Place the Brussels sprouts in a 2-quart saucepan. Add enough water to cover and bring to a full boil. Cook over medium heat until Brussels sprouts are crisply tender (12 to 15 minutes); drain. Return to pan; add remaining ingredients. Cook over medium heat, stirring occasionally, until heated through (4 to 6 minutes). Did I mention that my Monique likes ''sprouts'' because they are the same color as her favorite stuffed frog. Whatever works!

APPLE MACADAMIA NUT CAKE
(With Egg Nog Sauce)

4 cups cooking apples, peeled, cored and diced
1 3½-ounce jar macadamia nuts
2½ cups sugar
3 cups all-purpose flour
½ teaspoon salt
2 teaspoons baking soda

1 teaspoon ground nutmeg
1 teaspoon cinnamon
½ cup vegetable oil
½ cup orange juice
1½ teaspoons vanilla extract
2 eggs, well beaten

Preheat oven to 325°F.

Mix apples with nuts and sugar. Let stand for one hour, stirring frequently. Add dry ingredients to apple mixture, then add oil and orange juice, vanilla and eggs. Mix batter by hand. Pour into a greased and floured tube pan. Bake for 1½ hours. Turn out on a rack to cool.

Egg Nog Sauce

2 cups prepared egg nog
1 tablespoon cornstarch

2 tablespoons dark rum (optional)

Mix ingredients with a wire whisk in a 2-quart sauce pan over medium heat, stirring constantly. Bring to a boil and then cook 1 minute longer. Cool and refrigerate 1 hour. Serve egg nog sauce over cake. I plan to diet right after the holidays; how about you?

ORANGE POACHED PEARS

6 medium-size ripe pears
3 cups water
1 cup sugar
Juice of 2 lemons
1 whole cinnamon stick

½ cup brandy
Rind of 1 medium orange
5 whole cloves
Mint leaf for garnish

Peel pears, cut in half, and core. Combine water, sugar, and lemon juice in a Dutch oven. Bring to a boil over medium heat, stirring until sugar dissolves. Add pears, cover, reduce heat, and simmer 7 to 10 minutes or until tender. Add whole cloves, cinnamon stick, orange rind and brandy. Simmer an additional 5 minutes. Remove from heat. Transfer pears and liquid to a large bowl, cover, and chill thoroughly. To serve, remove pears from poaching liquid and place, core side up, on a large platter. Fill with rounded tablespoon orange cranberry sauce. (See page 55.)

GRANDMA PARENT'S HEAVENLY PIE

4 eggs, separated
1 pint heavy cream
1½ cup sugar
3 tablespoons lemon juice
¼ teaspoon cream of tartar

1 tablespoon grated lemon rind
⅛ teaspoon salt
1 tablespoon sugar
1 teaspoon vanilla extract

Preheat oven to 275°F.
Sift 1 cup of sugar with cream of tartar. Beat egg whites until stiff and gradually add sugar mixture. Spread mixture into bottom and side of a greased 10-inch Pyrex pie plate and bake for 1 hour. Let this crust cool. Beat egg yolks slightly. Stir in ½ cup sugar, lemon juice, grated lemon rind, and salt. Cook mixture in a double boiler 8-10 minutes, stirring occasionally. Cool. Whip 1 pint heavy cream with 1 tablespoon sugar and 1 teaspoon vanilla extract. Add ½ of this whipped cream to the cooled lemon mixture. Spread the other half of whipped cream on pie top and refrigerate for 1 hour.

Recipe for someone with a sweet tooth

Sing a song of mincemeat,
Currants, raisins, spice,
Apples, sugar, nutmeg,
Every thing that's nice.
Stir it with a ladle,
Wish a lovely wish,

Drop it in the middle
Of your well-filled dish.
Stir again for good luck,
Pack it all away
Tied in little jars and pots
Until Christmas Day

—ELIZABETH GOULD

The Days After Christmas

Christmas had been over for days, but my mother never seemed to notice. She stretched the season out, keeping her decorations up right through January. For her, the ones we had made always meant the most. No matter how late it was or how tired she might be, she always made time for us. I remember one evening in particular when my sister, brothers, and I were quite little. It was way past our bedtime, but she had let us stay up. "Children, come to the window," she called. "Have you ever seen the stars so clear and bright? Let's go out and get a better look." She lined us up on a sled and pulled us through the silent night all the way to the Common, just for a better look. Decades later, I remember her gift of the stars more than any other.

What I most enjoy about the days after Christmas

_____

_____

_____

_____

_____

Thoughts about the quiet moments we've always shared after Christmas

_____

_____

_____

_____

The first day back at school

_____

_____

_____

_____

I do hope your Christmas has had a little touch of Eternity in among the rush and pitter patter and all. It always seems such a mixing of this world and the next — but that after all is the idea!

— EVELYN UNDERHILL

Recipe Index